BLUFF YOUR WAY IN
BALLET

CRAIG DODD

D0289532

RAVETTE BOOKS

Published by Ravette Books Limited
3 Glenside Estate, Star Road,
Partridge Green, Horsham,
West Sussex RH13 8RA
(0403) 710392

First printed 1988
Updated and reprinted 1991

Series Editor – Anne Tauté

Cover design – Jim Wire
Typesetting – Input Typesetting Ltd.
Printing and binding – Cox & Wyman Ltd.
Production – Oval Projects Ltd.

The Bluffer's Guides are based on
an original idea by Peter Wolfe.

CONTENTS

Ballet Companies:

American Ballet Theatre	24
Australian Ballet	32
Ballet de Marseille	30
Ballet Rambert	31
Basel/Basle Ballet	33
Berlin Ballet, The	34
Bolshoi, The	22
English National Ballet	26
Kirov, The	23
London City Ballet	28
National Ballet of Canada	30
Nederlands Dans Theater	31
New York City Ballet	25
Paris Opéra Ballet	30
Royal Ballet, The	25
Royal Danish Ballet	28
Royal Swedish Ballet	29
Scottish Ballet	28
Stuttgart Ballet	33

INTRODUCTION
What is Ballet?

Ballet is simply formalised dancing, evolved over four centuries from court dance. It now bears roughly the sort of relationship to its origins that Fred Astaire and Ginger Rogers do to Ballroom dancing. Precious little.

Its terminology is French, coming from court dance and horse ballets. Its most obvious special feature is that ballerinas perform the totally unnatural feat of dancing on the tips of their toes. This is called dancing *en pointe*. As a result ballerinas' feet are not a pretty sight, and give chiropodists a field day.

Ballet roughly divides into three compartments.

1. **Classical** is the purest form of ballet based on the grand Russian style of the 19th century, though the French may have views on this. It is seen at its purest in the great classic ballets such as *Swan Lake* or *The Sleeping Beauty*.

2. **Neo-classical** is very much identified with the work of choreographer Balanchine starting in the late 1920s when he transformed his classical training at the Imperial Ballet of the Tsar into a personal style, in ballets such as *Apollo*. He went on to create many other plotless pure-dance works. In recent years neo-classicism has often come to mean old ballets in new leotards.

3. **Modern Ballet** is simply the classical vocabulary of steps distorted in any way to express what a particular choreographer wants. This can encompass the sexual contortions of Béjart, the athleticism of Kylian or the jazz inspired works of Alvin Ailey, but is not to be confused with modern dance which is a different kettle of *poisson* and not within the scope of this definitive volume.

HOW TO ENJOY BALLET

The best advice a bluffer can offer to anyone with a mental block about ballet is that they should to just sit back and enjoy it. Thinking at the ballet is not to be encouraged. The most frequent complaint heard about ballet is 'I don't know what it means', said by people with the mistaken belief that anyone actually involved in the business does.

Ballet has been described as a dangerous art, very seductive and liable to arouse previously hidden emotions. Let's face it, ballet is a physical business and, to put it bluntly, sexual. Anyone who pretends they like a particular dancer purely for their *arabesque* is talking tosh. Looks come into it too, and anyone who says otherwise is being economical with the truth. A pretty face (on either sex) can make up for lots of technical faults. A brilliant technician, on the other hand, may have to battle the way to the top if less than moderately good looking.

Mime

Mime can be the great hang-up for the beginner and is yet another reason for people to complain that they don't understand ballet. This is hard to credit as ballet mime is so simple-minded it makes charades seem like nuclear physics.

If the Princess Mother in *Swan Lake* points to her ring finger you can safely guess she's telling Siegfried it's time to wed and not admiring her nail polish. The same goes for Aurora in *The Sleeping Beauty* who quite clearly has four princes waiting to woo her.

Hands swirled above the head, like mixing pastry, means dance. Admittedly this may not be immediately obvious, but as dancing invariably takes place thereafter it's not a matter of immediate concern.

Hands placed on the chest indicate love, not indigestion. A raised arm giving a two-finger salute (fingers together, boy-scout fashion) swears that the love will be eternal. Experienced bluffers will know that this means some serious two-timing is in the offing.

In one or two of the big story ballets there are longer passages of mime which no-one really understands without a programme note. On first viewing you should not feel left out if you do not realise that the Swan Queen is explaining that the lake is made from her mothers' tears or that Giselle's mother is telling the yokels that the local woods are haunted by the spirits of girls who died after being jilted. It won't spoil overall enjoyment of the ballet if you have a brief nap while this is going on. It's all in the music anyway.

Name-calling

It is essential to be aware of the right mode of address when discussing people in the ballet. The correct use of dancers' and choreographers' names can suggest greater knowledge of the ballet world; indeed, even intimacy with some of its inhabitants.

Dancers tend to be called by their Christian names. Diminutives are used rarely, unless the dancer is Russian, when it is almost obligatory. Choreographers or directors are invariably called by their surnames.

A few examples. Anthony Dowell is currently director of the Royal Ballet. He is also a principal dancer. So it is in order to say after a performance "Wasn't Anthony absolutely fabulous tonight?" "Tony was marvellous" just wouldn't do. You could then go on to say "Dowell should give him some new roles." But if you were talking about Natalia Makarova the opening sentence would go "Wasn't *Natasha* absolutely fabulous tonight?"

The assiduous bluffer will soon pick up the names in common usage. There are a few exceptions, usually involving the all-time greats who have become much-loved fixtures and fittings of the ballet world. An Ashton ballet may be announced, but ballet bluffers refer to it as one by "Sir Fred". And Balanchine may have been an institution, but "Mr.B" did the daily work. Dame Ninette de Valois created the Royal Ballet but "Madam" ran it for over 30 years.

In at least one area of ballet, life has become easier for the bluffer. The use of backstage camp names within companies is on the wane. A whole generation of Dorises, Monas, and Hetties are now distinguished gentlemen, teaching or directing ballet companies.

Who's Who

The ballet world is inhabited by a curious set of deeply inter-dependent people. Some are actively involved, others strictly on the sidelines. Here are a few tips on how to spot them.

Insiders include . . .

The Artistic Director

The Artistic Director is usually a choreographer or dancer either retired or, quite often these days, still dancing. More often than not they are budding megalomaniacs who listen to no-one, ruining careers at whim, often under the mistaken belief they are helping them. Bluffers should remember that the greatest artistic director was **Diaghilev** who did not choreograph, dance, design or compose. Nowadays companies cannot afford this luxury and actually expect some work from the director. Other than acting like god, they usually make ballets or, if they are still dancing, hog the best roles for themselves.

The Choreographer

These are the men and women who create the ballets; not just the steps, but the whole production. With varying degrees of success they choose the story, the music and the designer. Between nervous breakdowns and creative crises they spend most of their time trying to convince everyone except themselves that they know what they are doing. They are the most important people in the company, as everyone else from the dancers to the stage staff, designers and ultimately the administrative staff, depend upon their creativity. All, that is, except the musicians, who have such a stranglehold on the theatre that even if there is no work they can still turn up and get paid.

The Music Director/Conductor

The conductor has the thankless task of trying to get a passable result out of the musicians. They in turn have the thankless task of playing a lot of ballet music which, musically speaking, can leave a lot to be desired. The conductor should have some rapport with the dancers, but often he buries his head in the score and ignores what is happening on the stage. Great conductors who demean themselves with the occasional ballet performance will all too often play at their own tempo, usually more suited to a concert performance, leaving the dancers to cope as best they can. If it doesn't look good, the dancer gets the blame and the conductor gets the good reviews. Orchestral playing for ballet very often leaves much to be desired which is not always the fault of the conductor. In opera house companies it has been known for the conductor to have a good rehearsal with the orchestra in the morning, only to turn up for the evening performance and hardly recognise a face in the orchestra pit. For reasons losts in the mists of time and union negotiations, musicians are allowed to nominate deputies if they have something better to do. Why this is allowed to happen is a major mystery of the ballet world.

The Pianist

The person who plays for the daily ballet class, as well as rehearsals. They have to possess the patience of Job to play fairly nondescript music for class and then spend the rest of the day endlessly repeating phrases of music for rehearsals. On top of this they have to cope with the whims of dancers and choreographers, which led one pianist to cry 'How do you want it today. Too slow or too fast?'

Ballet Master/Mistress

The person who really runs the ballet company day-by-day. This post is often held by a dancer put out to grass and is thus in a position to settle old scores by influencing the casting of roles, usually to the benefit of their (temporary) favourites. Supervising endless rehearsals and teaching dancers new roles takes infinite patience, an eagle eye and endless packets of cigarettes.

Notators

The people who write down the ballets in strange hieroglyphics on music paper; the most widely-used system is called choreology, invented by Joan and

Rudolf Benesh. It's so widely-used that notators are invariably called choreologists. They are the guardians of the holy writ, the bible in which ballets are written down and which is consulted during rehearsals.

Dancers

If bluffers mingle with dancers they will soon find that there is only one topic of conversation – the dancers themselves. It's best not to try to bluff your way with a dancer as they have invariably lived and breathed ballet from a very early age and rarely know nor care about anything else. There is little you can say to impress a dancer other than to offer to buy dinner.

Fortunately dancers can be spotted a mile off by their turned-out feet and the inevitable dance bag slung over their shoulder – invariably Gucci or Louis Vuitton even for the lowliest member of the corps de ballet. All are striking to look at no matter how genuinely good or bad looking they are. They all know how to wear clothes with effect. Though most can make the contents of an Oxfam shop look the height of fashion they tend to be members of the Designer Tendency, with special interest in the leather and suede departments. Conservationists fear for the lives of herds of animals which have to be slaughtered annually to dress leading dancers.

Surprisingly many dancers smoke. Marlboro is the brand leader and they smoke them by the packet. Though some companies have declared studios smoke free zones they seem to have had little effect on total consumption. Ashtrays make a convenient missile for choreographers to heave around at trying moments.

Life in a ballet company is very incestuous with dancers having affairs or marrying each other in infinite combinations. A few form relationships outside the ballet world, but the nature of ballet life, rehearsing together all day and performing together every evening, makes this difficult. A few spectacular break-outs in recent years have included marriages to a Sainsbury, a Marquess and a clutch of merchant bankers. Two Royal Ballet ballerinas have even been married to ballet critics. Indeed, one still is.

Dancers live in an hierarchical world. At the top of the pile is that rare creature, the **prima ballerina assoluta**, only one or two a lifetime, which can be quite enough. Some like **Margot Fonteyn** are charm itself, but others like **Mathilde Kshessinska** seem to have read far more into the title than was ever intended. The male equivalent doesn't technically exist, but several dancers seem to think it does to judge by their off-stage behaviour.

The next category down is the plain **ballerina** or **principal dancer**, those who really head companies and dance the lion's share of the major roles.

Waiting in the wings and eager to share those roles are the **soloists** who do even more work, as they must be able to step in for an indisposed principal or corps de ballet member.

Just below the soloists come the **coryphees**, a term which, in translation from the Greek can mean either a leading dancer in a ballet or a chorus member. This aptly defines the no-man's land they inhabit having graduated from the corps de ballet, but not quite made it to soloists. Dancers can languish in this limbo for years.

At the bottom of the pile are the unsung heroes and heroines of the ballet, the **corps de ballet**. They are destined to appear in almost every ballet grasping at any tiny opportunity to shine and catch a choreographer's eye. But all too often they are left standing around as human scenery with fixed smiles on their faces trying to convince themselves and the audience that their years of expensive and dedicated training are being put to good use.

The Real VIP's

While the inward-looking ballet world dances in ever-decreasing circles, the really important people devotedly buy tickets (except for critics who get them for nothing) at ever-increasing prices.

These long suffering outsiders include. . . .

Balletomanes

Not all ballet lovers are balletomanes. As the title implies they are the dedicated groupies of the dance world, for whom dance is the world. The species is often recognised by its outfits; for the males, tweedy jackets over a cosy woolly, baggy trousers and, in extreme cases, sandals; for the females a 'cardie' draped over shoulders, a cotton print dress and flat shoes. These are dedicated people and any spare cash goes on tickets.

Trying to bluff your way with a balletomane is a fool venture as they know everything, particularly about their favourite dancers. They know all the current gossip about ballet personalities and politics and, if over a certain age, are sure to have seen **Ulanova** dance Giselle in 1956 and hanker after a golden age of ballet when all dancers were greater artistes than those on the stage today.

Should you accidentally fall into conversation with a balletomane make some quick excuse to get yourself to the other end of the bar as soon as possible.

The main function of a true balletomane is to massage the ego of dancers by sending cards and small presents on opening nights and waiting outside stage doors in all weathers to present flowers or collect autographs.

Ballet Mothers

Ballet mothers are not recognised by any outward feature, but only by the glazed look on the eyes of those to whom they are talking. They are invariably singing the praises of their talented offspring and lamenting how artistic directors just do not seem to appreciate that talent. In fact they do, all too well, which is why they insist on casting the talented offspring as one of Juliet's friends, while Juliet is danced by some truly talented 16-year-old.

On no account humour a ballet mother out of kindness as this will guarantee that the next time your paths cross she will bear straight down on you, certain of a fair, unbiased, hearing. Escape to the other end of the bar is not advised in this case as she is sure to follow. Simply wave at some mythical friend in the crowd and disappear into it.

The original ballet mum was probably Catherine de Medici – see Terrine de Ballet.

Critics

These men and women who review ballet performances for the national and provincial press speak a language of their own, largely for their own benefit or for the hordes of dancers who swear that they *never* read reviews.

Critics usually sit in aisle seats to effect hasty exits at the end of performances, ostensibly to get to their telephones or newspapers quickly. In practice this arrangement merely gets them to the free interval drinks or to the bar ahead of anyone else. It can be

educational for a crafty bluffer to eavesdrop in the bar
and hear the truly bitchy comments that are said about
performances, but never appear in print.

How to Translate a Ballet Review

Bluffers should remember that critics hunt in packs.
Careful reading, usually between the lines, will reveal
pack leaders and camp followers. Astute bluffers will
soon learn to recognise that if the Daily Bugle likes a
performance, the Daily Thunderer is likely to approve
as well. But, just as night follows day, the Evening
Crier and the Evening Bystander will dislike it.
Careful observation can therefore greatly reduce a
ballet bluffer's newspaper bill. Look out for the
following phrases.

Promising – Suggests much, but is rarely fulfilled.
Many dancers remain promising until retirement.

Dependable – An over-30-year-old who was once
promising.

Coped well with the technical demands – Fell over,
but is a long-time favourite of the critic.

Partnered strongly – Threw the ballerina round with
excessive force.

Partnered tentatively – Dropped the ballerina.

Dazzling technique – Flashy steps at the expense of
all else.

Sensitive artistry – Simpered excessively. The
French and Italians excel at this.

Well-schooled – Dull.

Innovative choreography – Obscure or downright
perverse.

Avant-garde choreography – Something supported by the Arts Council entirely for the benefit of the choreographer involved.

Enfant terrible of ballet – Terribly childish choreographer.

Interesting interpretation – The critic had no clue what the dancer was doing.

Let the role speak through the steps – The dancer couldn't act for toffee.

A triumph of acting ability – The dancer couldn't dance for toffee.

Made his or her presence felt – Upstaged everyone else.

Guest artiste – Either an expensive import, or the company humouring an old dancer doing a bit part.

Lively tempo – The orchestra managed to keep well ahead of the dancers.

Triple-bill – Three short ballets with two long intervals. The Royal Ballet are the market leaders in this department.

Gala evening – Odds and ends of ballets the company couldn't make a regular evening of.

Royal gala – As above, but at higher prices, and graced by a minor royal of Danish or Austrian origin.

Invaluable programme notes – The ballet was unintelligible. Or the critic wrote the synopsis.

Terpsichorean Technique

A basic knowledge of ballet technique is essential for the ballet bluffer as no conversation is complete without a sprinkling of technical terms. This is not as daunting as it sounds as you do not actually have to know too much about the steps. It suffices to know that certain dancers are particularly remembered for certain things (Svetlana's *arabesque*, John's *attitude*, etc.) and that the number of basic steps is limited anyway. All bluffers should learn to recognise the 'Fred step' which is the trademark of Sir Fred's ballets, rather like Alfred Hitchcock's cameo appearances in his films.

Technique has evolved over the centuries from the first mincing steps of dancers at the French court. The bluffer need know only the few key steps and the people most associated with them.

La Camargo introduced the *entrechat quatre* in the early 1700s and to do so shortened her skirt. The German ballerina Anna Heinel introduced the *pirouette a la seconde* in the late 1700s. The beginning of the 19th century saw the ballerina tentatively rising on to *pointe* and by the mid-1800s technique was becoming stronger. By the late 1800s ballerinas were firmly on *pointe* and able to do multiple *pirouettes*, notably the famous 32 *fouettés* which were first performed by Pierina Legnani in *Cinderella* in 1893. She repeated the feat as Odile, the Black Swan in *Swan Lake* in 1895 which is where we see them today.

After the precocity of Louis XIV, the Sun King, male technique reached a peak at the end of the 1700s with the arrival on the dance scene of Gaetano Vestris, the 'God of the Dance' and his son, Auguste, who inherited the title. He had great *elevation* and could perform both *pirouettes* and *entrechats*. Male technique then went into decline with the male dancer acting as little more than a porter (*porteur* if the bluffer has to be absolutely correct) carrying the ballerina around, until the arrival of ten-year-old Vaslav Nijinsky at the Imperial School of Ballet in St Petersburg in 1898.

From this point technique develops at an alarming rate achieving almost circus-trick proportions at times. The average principal dancer today has to perform feats which probably match anything Nijinsky did – and to have a better shape as well.

Glossary of Ballet Terms

Adage – The slow bit which starts a *pas de deux* and is followed by two solos and a coda. Also exercises done in slow tempo.

Allegro – The part of a ballet class made up of fast steps, beats, jumps or turns, and not the only make of car a coryphee can afford.

Arabesque – A pose on one leg with the other leg raised back, the body and arms making a complementary line.

Attitude – Often struck by dancers. Based on the statue of Mercury by Bologna, the dancer stands on one leg with the other raised behind, with the knee bent and the corresponding arm raised.

Ballet blanc – White ballets like *Les Sylphides* or the second act of *Giselle*.

Ballon – Having the attributes of a balloon, in bounce (but not in shape).

Barre – What dancers lean on for support on and off stage.

Battement – Beating movements of the legs performed at the barre.

Batterie – Steps in which the feet beat together or cross when in the air and not the place in which the Golden Cockerel was raised.

Bourrée, pas de – The linking steps performed by the Queen of the Wilis in *Giselle* which make her appear to glide across the stage.

Cabriole – A jumping step in which the dancer raises one leg, bringing the other sharply up to beat with it. Dancers who excel at them can be said to have cabriole legs.

Chat, pas de – A light jumping step, sideways, like a cat.

Coupé jeté – Turning jumps from one foot to the other encircling the stage and not a fast car.

Entrechat – The step everyone knows because of its funny name. The dancer jumps in the air and crosses the feet. Bluffers should beware that *entrechats* are numbered, not according to the number of times the feet cross, but the number of changes of position of the feet from ground to ground. An **entrechat dix** has been performed (the feet crossing five times) but it all happens so fast that the dancer looks like a mad gnat in the air. You are not expected to keep count.

Fouetté – The second most famous ballet step in which the ballerina (usually) whips herself into a frenzy of turns. *Fouetté* is French for whip. Get it?

Gargouillade – Not much call for this term, but bluffers might like to know that Dame Marie Rambert called it 'gargling with your feet'. It's like a *pas de chat* with a *rond de jambe* thrown in for good measure.

Jeté – Means thrown, but is in fact a jump, though

the way some dancers throw themselves into a jump makes it a reasonably accurate term.

Manège – Not a step, but the circular pattern on the stage in which virtuoso jumps are performed.

Pas – As in *de deux, de quatre*, means simply, step.

Piqué – Not a mood the ballerina finds herself in, but when she steps directly on to *pointe* without bending the knee or going through the foot – that's **relevé**.

Pirouette – Turn, but not as in 'I've had a nasty turn', though some dancers do have that effect on the audience when they do them.

Plié – From the French for fold and not for plaice (see *poisson*). The first exercises at the barre, slowly bending the knees and lowering the body, in the five positions.

Pointe – Standing on the tip of the toe. What ballet is about to most people and what it lacks to others.

Poisson – What it says, fish. A jump with the body arched backwards like a fish jumping out of water is a *temps de poisson*. When the ballerina is caught in this position, as in *Sleeping Beauty*, it is a fish dive or, to be correct, *pas poisson*.

Ports de bras – How dancers carry their arms and not a chest support.

Positions – The five basic turned-out positions of the feet and their related arm movements.

Rond de jambe – Could be a ham sandwich, specially as they feature heavily in Danish ballets. The leg is raised with a bent knee. The pointed toe then describes a circle in the air.

Tour en l'air – Mainly performed by men, a jump in

the air with a single, double or sometimes triple turn thrown in.

Turn-out – a) The size of the audience, b) The turn-out of the legs from the hips and not, as bluffers should be aware, from the knees or ankles.

A Dangerous Obsession

Meet a dancer off-stage and the chances are they're 'off', suffering from stress-fractures, hairline fractures, brain fractures, or merely self-imposed anorexia. Bluffers might well wonder why any normal person would take up a career which has so many walking wounded.

Throughout history there have been accidents. A candle started a fire when Dauberval was dancing. Fellow dancer Dangui, three tailors and six stage-hands died, and Mlle Guimard, naked, grilled in her dressing room until a stagehand wrapped her in a curtain for her escape. Emma Livry, Taglioni's protégé, was not so lucky. Her dress caught fire from a gas-jet and she died a lingering death.

Quick thinking by dancers has saved situations; a ballerina whose nose was disjointed by a blow from her partner had it quickly knocked straight by fellow ballerina Freya Dominic; Michael Ho's knee was snapped back into place by a dancer on stage. And the audience didn't notice.

The audience did notice 17-year-old Fred Sharp's debut as an extra in *Romeo and Juliet* with the Joffrey Ballet. He fell ten feet through a trap-door and was then hit on the head by a candelabra in Juliet's funeral procession. He lived.

BALLET COMPANIES

Ballet companies have personalities just as much as dancers, sometimes reflecting their history, sometimes that of their founder. True bluffers should have a little knowledge of the background and flavour of major companies to avoid any obvious mistakes. For example no true ballet bluffer would openly admit to admiring Maurice Béjart's Ballet of the Twentieth Century without a well-practised sneer at the same time; no true bluffer would think that a reference to 'City Ballet' referred to any other city than New York, no matter how highly they think of London City Ballet.

Companies have their ups and downs and the wheel of fortune can have the Royal Ballet riding high in critical acclaim one season and being criticised unmercifully the next for little apparent reason other than that the real focus of interest has moved, say, to a revitalised London Festival Ballet. But all companies live with the knowledge that the wheel keeps on turning. . .

The Bolshoi

Bolshoi means big and that's the way they dance, though the name actually refers to the theatre. If bluffers want to go over the top praising their athletic, bravura style, they are advised always to suggest a sneaking preference for the pure classicism of the Kirov.

Though there has been ballet at the Bolshoi since the 1770s its present-day style is very much the product of the Russian Revolution. Fortunately the first Commissar of Enlightenment allowed productions of the classics which were officially frowned upon as a hangover of the Tsar and his court. The first Soviet ballet was *The Red Poppy*, the story of a Chinese dancer who saves the life of a Soviet ship's captain who brought grain to her land during a coolie uprising. Pure poetry. Since then the Bolshoi have specialised in epic, full-length productions. Their first appearance in the West in 1956 was a milestone of ballet history; the performances by Ulanova and Fadeyechev in *Romeo and Juliet* a milestone in the roster of great ballet performances. It is essential for the bluffer to at least have seen this on film in order to make suitable comments. Later epics have included *Spartacus* by the company's director Grigorovich. The Bolshoi is currently on an upswing.

The Kirov

Always had a superior air to the Bolshoi. Truly regarded as the home of the Imperial Ballet when it was called the Maryinsky (bluffers should take care to refer to Maryinsky style, rather than Kirov style on occasions such as when discussing the works of Balanchine or the heritage of the Royal Ballet). The home of the classical style which is the basis of all the 20th-century companies in the West, Mikhail Fokine created half-a-dozen ballets at the Maryinsky before he left after the Revolution. The Soviet authorities asked him again to stay, but he opted for the West. The most important person after Fokine's departure was the eminent teacher Vaganova, after whom the Kirov School was renamed in 1957. The theatre itself only became the Kirov in 1935, in memory of the head of the Leningrad Communist Party who had been assassinated.

July 1961 brought the Kirov to the West; an unforgettable occasion when 32 perfectly-schooled Kirov ballerinas slowly came on stage doing *penchée arabesque* after *penchée arabesque* until it was filled for the beginning of the Kingdom of the Shades act of *La Bayadère*.

The Kirov, unlike the Bolshoi, has suffered serious defections; Nureyev, Makarova and Baryshnikov left for greater artistic freedom and choice of designer clothes. After a minor identity crisis is reasserting itself and forging links with Western dancers and companies such as the Berlin Ballet.

American Ballet Theatre*

When Natasha and Misha (Makarova and Baryshnikov) defected it was to ABT, as the company is always known, that they fled. To audiences across America this is considered the 'national' company as it has always toured extensively, bringing many other foreign dancers to its audience. These have included Alicia and Pat (Markova and Dolin) during the Second World War and after; Erik and Carla (Bruhn and Fracci); and a host of others. They gave a stage to Antony Tudor who created many of his great works for them, as well as to the modern choreographer, Twyla Tharp. ABT recently poached MacMillan (Sir Kenneth) from the Royal Ballet as principal choreographer and he took Alex (Alessandra Ferri) with him.

ABT have a basic repertoire of the classics, including Baryshnikov's *Cinderella*, which is allegedly the most expensive production ever. The company has been in the news more for management disputes than its performances, with dancers such as Fernando (Bujones), Cynthia (Gregory) and Gelsey (Kirkland) coming and going like yoyos. With Baryshnikov's departure as director, Hollywood bound, the company is yet again marking time.

* Wary bluffers will note the spelling.

New York City Ballet

Always referred to as City Ballet. Very much the personal empire of George Balanchine and Lincoln Kirstein, who invited him to America in 1935. They first formed the School of American Ballet, which still largely supplies the company with thoroughbred ballerinas in the Balanchine mould – long-legged beauties with doe eyes, hair scraped back severely and thin, very thin. One-time Ballanchine ballerina, Gelsey Kirkland, has documented in painful detail the agonies some dancers go through to get that way: uppers and downers and other methods, some not entirely fit for polite society to discuss.

The company was formed in 1948 and is now based at the State Theater, Lincoln Center, New York. After Balanchine's death in 1985 it was directed by one of his oldest collaborators, Jerome Robbins, and one of his star dancers, Peter Martins. Now Martins alone has taken charge of its fortunes, giving himself and young dancers the chance to step into Mr. B's choreographic shoes. A fairly hopeless task, but one providing interest for bluffers.

The Royal Ballet

Many foreigners think it a total conceit that this company is so named, assuming everyone should know where it comes from. It wasn't even the first ballet company to be given a Royal Charter; the Royal Winnipeg had theirs three years earlier.

The Royal Ballet was founded by Dame Ninette de Valois. Bluffers must always refer to her as Madam, as does everyone else. She started by producing dances for Lilian Baylis at the Old Vic Theatre, and then formed a school at the Sadler's Wells Theatre. Its growth provides good bluffing material. In the beginning the Vic-Wells (1931) begat the Sadler's Wells Ballet (1940) begat the Sadler's Wells Theatre Ballet (1945) which, on receipt of a Royal Charter in 1956, begat The Royal Ballet. This in turn begat several variations on a Sadler's Wells Royal Ballet theme, culminating with the Birmingham Royal Ballet. Meanwhile, *The* Royal Ballet remains at Covent Garden.

Madam directed the company until 1963, to be succeeded by Sir Fred, then Sir Kenneth (for a time with John Field), then Morrice (formerly of Ballet Rambert) and now Anthony Dowell.

The company is the guardian of the priceless Ashton repertoire (though some bluffers might find this guardianship a bit wanting at times), has the major MacMillan ballets, an international selection ranging from Robbins to Kylian, with the classics in productions which have been received with varying degrees of hostility, particularly Dowell's gloriously over-designed *Swan Lake*.

The roster of great ballerinas of the company's past including Moira Shearer, Beryl Grey, Nadia Nerina, Svetlana Beriosova, Park, Seymour and Sibley has, for most bluffers, a mixture of glamour and authority that is only just being regained by young dancers such as Viviane Durante and Darcey Bussell. Supreme stood Dame Margot Fonteyn, muse of Ashton.

Great male dancers with the company have included Helpmann, Somes, Blair, Wall, Gable and Dowell. A bright new generation including Pickford, Sansom and Cassidy have been joined by Mukhamedov from the Bolshoi. Bluffers will soon be on first name terms with them.

English National Ballet

(formerly London Festival Ballet)

Festival Ballet was founded by Alicia (now Dame) Markova and Anton (later Sir Anton) Dolin with a brilliant impresario, Dr Julian Braunsweg, whose scurrilous memoirs are a good source for bluffers. Later directors included Donald Alberry and John Gilpin (the brilliant ballet classicist), Beryl Grey, John Field and Peter Schaufuss, the most charismatic occupant of the post. His ousting caused national headlines and he was immediately snapped up by the Berlin Ballet. The current director is Ivan Nagy. Dedicated bluffers should know the correct way to pronounce his name – Narge, though purists will insist on using the Hungarian, Nodge.

Festival Ballet (named in 1950 for the impending Festival of Britain) introduced many great foreign dancers such as Toumanova and Danilova, Toni Lander from Denmark, and, more recently, Samsova from Russia and Terabust from Italy, as well as Eva Evdokimova, the company's greatest Sylph. Home-grown ballerinas are a rarity, but have included Belinda Wright who inherited Markova's position in 1952, Gaye Fulton and André Hall, who is now with the Berlin Ballet. Natalia Makarova has danced a notable Tatiana in *Onegin* and produced the company's *Swan Lake*.

Male dancers in the early years included Dolin and Gilpin as well as Flemming Flindt and André Prokovsky (both now prolific choreographers), Georges Goviloff and Patrice Bart. Peter Schaufuss was a principal for many years and produced the company's definitive version of *La Sylphide*. He also acquired two 'lost' ballets of Sir Fred's, *Romeo and Juliet* and *Apparitions,* the latter soon returning to oblivion.

Scottish Ballet

Based in Glasgow, 'Scottish' was very much the creation
of Peter Darrell after the demise of his (and Liz West's)
Western Theatre Ballet. Some of his socially-aware
ballets remain (subjects range from incest to homo-
sexuality), including *Swan Lake* in which the 'white'
acts are a drug-induced fantasy. Elaine MacDonald, his
ballerina and one-time associate director of the company, is one of Britain's greatest dramatic ballerinas.
Current director Galina Samsova is strengthening the
company's classical base, as bluffers would expect from
such an oustanding ballerina.

London City Ballet

Dogged determination by founder Harold King has
kept this little company on the road, unsubsidised and
largely unsung.

Royal Danish Ballet

Summing up 250 years of history would be difficult for
bluffers were it not for the name 'Bournonville'. For
150 of those years the man and then his influence have
meant Danish ballet. He not only created the ballets
which are the mainstay of the repertoire, but also
defined the style of dancing in which they are
performed. Auguste Bournonville took over as director,
choreographer, dancer and social conscience in 1829,
giving up the dancing in 1848, but continuing the
other posts in the style of an absolute monarch until
1875. Of the 50 or so ballets he created a surprisingly
high number remain in the repertoire, notably *La
Sylphide, Napoli, Folk Tale, Kermesse in Bruges* and
Konservatoriet.

The Royal Danish is notable for producing fine male dancers; Bournonville made dancing a respectable occupation, something which has yet to happen in many countries. Over recent years these have included Erik Bruhn, Henning Kronstam, Niels Kehlet, Flemming Flindt, Peter Martins, Peter Schaufuss and Ib Andersen. Ballerinas have included Margot Lander, Toni Lander, Mona Vangsaae, Anna Laerkesen and, presently, Lis Jeppeson, their great Sylph. Vangsaae and Kronstam enter the ballet history books as Ashton's Romeo and Juliet.

Latest in the line of directors, which has included Harald Lander (creator of *Etudes*), Niels Bjorn Larsen (ballet's greatest mime), Frank Schaufuss, Flindt and Kronstam, is Frank Andersen. Bluffers will realise that with the number of Danish dancers leaving to dance abroad, and the lack of a great ballerina, the company can only mark time at present.

Royal Swedish Ballet

Rarely venturing abroad (the dancers can't bear the inconvenience) this company has produced many fine dancers and has an excellent repertoire, ranging from Antony Tudor (who directed the company for four years from 1949) to Robbins, alongside the classics which include Beryl Grey's production of *The Sleeping Beauty*. Stockholm-based dancers are virtually unknown on the international circuit, including their beautiful ballerina Anneli Alhanko (Finnish actually) and handsome leading man Per-Arthur Segerstrom. Dancers to look out for abroad are Johann Renvall with ABT, Tim Almaas with ENB, Anders Hellstrom in Hamburg, Petter Jacobsson with the BRB and Matz Skoog. At home a new generation, largely from the RSB school are truly outstanding. Watch out for Goran Svalberg (whose father directs the school) and Anders Nordstrom.

National Ballet of Canada

Founded by Celia Franca on the recommendation of Madam in 1951. Based in Toronto where it has fine studios and a large school which produces most of its yearly intake of dancers. Headed for some years by Canada's national treasure, Karen Kain, partnered by Frank Augustyn, the company has in turn been directed by David Haber (briefly), Alexander Grant (controversially) and Erik Bruhn. After his death Valerie Wilder and Lynn Wallis took over.

Attempts to develop a 'Canadian' choreographic image have not been fruitful and the repertoire is based on the classics, including Nureyev's *The Sleeping Beauty* which almost bankrupted them and Peter Schaufuss's *Napoli* which would have done, had it not been so successful. Grant gambled and it paid off, placing NBC more firmly on the international stage. In 1987 the company dived down a rabbit hole after Glen Tetley's *Alice* and bluffers can only hope they emerge unscathed under current director, Reid Anderson.

Paris Opéra Ballet

In the 30s, 40s and into the 50s run by Serge Lifar, with Yvette Chauvire as prima ballerina. Directed controversially in recent years by Nureyev who produced highly idiosyncratic ballets before a much-publicised row which led to his departure. He was touring America in *The King and I* at the time. The school continues to produce outstanding, if occasionally flashy, dancers.

Ballet de Marseille

The creation of Roland Petit has all the show-biz flair associated with this most French-of-French choreographers. Though the company tours a lot, Petit ballets don't travel well and are rarely successful when danced by other companies. Petit's wife, Zizi Jeanmaire, still appears occasionally in ballets such as *The Bat* in which she is the epitome of French style. Dominique Khalfouni and Denys Ganio are the company's principals; the only couple who can perform Petit's *Carmen* with style sufficient to blow away the smell of 1940s mothballs. Petit's style is dancing chic, too chic.

Nederlands Dans Theater

One of the most influential modern dance companies. Founded in 1959 by a group from the Dutch National Ballet including Benjamin Harkavy and Hans van Manen. Now based in the Hague and directed by the Czech choreographer and mushroom-fancier, Jiri Kylian. Though modern dance in outlook, its training is firmly classical. It has produced many powerful dancers including Alexandra Radius and Han Ebbelaar who went on to become principals of the Dutch National. Still producing more new works a season than any other company, its smaller company, (NDT2), under Arlette van Boven, produced a new generation of choreographers. Watch out for Natcho Duarte. The company mushrooms; there is now NDT3.

Ballet Rambert

Listed under this name for sentimental reasons. From 1987 its new name is Rambert Dance Company, which reflects their dance style more accurately. The child of the formidable Marie Rambert, Polish dancer with Diaghilev, who admitted to being in love with Nijinsky when she helped to mount *The Rite of Spring*. She married the British playwright Ashley Dukes in 1918 and opened a studio in London in 1920. The Marie Rambert Dancers, which became the Ballet Rambert and the Ballet Club, gave their first performance in 1930 at the tiny, but famous, Mercury Theatre. Bluffers will recognise it (and a brief glimpse of Mim, as Marie Rambert was known) in *The Red Shoes*.

While Madam was creating what would become the 'national' British company, Rambert was discovering dancers and choreographers, including Ashton, Tudor, Howard, Gore and Staff. The indomitable Mim kept the company going until 1966 in spite of having no theatre of its own and with lack of a suitable theatre and a shortage of new post-war choreographic talent. In the end the huge cost of mounting classics which were the company's mainstay forced it to re-form, based on the model of Nederlands Dans Theater. In its modern re-incarnation Rambert enthusiastically encouraged American choreographers such as Tetley, as well as Norman Morrice and Christopher Bruce. Of uncertain direction in recent years, with clashes of directional ambitions, Robert North's term came to an end, to be succeeded by Eton-educated choreographer, Richard Alston. Floreat Rambert Dance Company.

Australian Ballet

Today's company is the successor of several from the 1940s formed largely by dancers from various Ballet Russe companies who settled there. When the founder of the Borovansky Ballet died in 1959, Peggy van Praagh (later Dame) was invited to take over. Bluffers might spot Madam's influence again. The first performance of the newly formed Australian Ballet was in November 1962. The repertoire reflected the strong Royal Ballet connections with ballets by Ashton and Cranko. In 1964 Robert Helpmann, himself an Australian, created *The Display* a ballet about the mating habits of the male lyre-bird. Perfect for Australian male dancers. In the same year a school was opened which eventually produced principal dancers such as Marilyn Rowe and John Meehan. Helpmann became associate director in 1965, taking over the reins completely in 1974. Following his retirement in 1976 Anne Woolliams, head of the school, took over. The company is now directed by Maina Gielgud, niece of Sir John, after a career as ballerina with Béjart and London Festival Ballet.

Very big down-under, the company merits greater exposure; but they are such a long way away from everywhere except New Zealand. Under Gielgud's direction they have added to their international repertoire ballets by Jiri Kylian and Glen Tetley as well as new works by Graeme Murphy of the Sydney Dance Company. To celebrate Australia's bi-centenary in 1988 they were transported back to Covent Garden. Next period of parole, London Coliseum, 1992.

Basel/Basle Ballet

Bluffers should know about this enterprising company and its enterprising ex-choreographer, Heinz Spoerli. His much-praised version of *La Fille Mal Gardée* has also been produced at the Paris Opéra. The company's most popular ballet is, not surprisingly, *Swiss Cheese*.

Stuttgart Ballet

Deserving a listing for past glories, mostly created by John Cranko for his muse, Marcia Haydée, and her American partner, Richard Cragun. *Onegin, Taming of the Shrew* and *Romeo and Juliet* are widely performed outside Germany. Glen Tetley briefly took over direction after Cranko's untimely death in 1973 and the company is now in the hands of Haydée. It is difficult to recreate the heady days of its founder, when Stuttgart was known as Cranko's Castle.

The Berlin Ballet

The arrival of Peter Schaufuss in Berlin galvanised a sleeping giant. Links were forged with the Kirov and a major new production of *Giselle* greeted with acclamation, making young Lisa Cullum from New Zealand a name to drop. Based at the Deutsche Oper, the company plans three major Tchaikovsky productions to mark the centenary of his death in 1993. The London Friends of Berlin Ballet (a mine of information for bluffers) hosts workshops with dancers such as Leanne Benjamin and Martin (mega-jump) James. *The* company to watch.

The Rest

This list inevitably leaves out many companies. In **America** there are dozens of regional companies of note, such as Pittsburgh, Boston and San Francisco. The regional companies of **Russia,** such as Perm, produce spectacular dancers who eventually find their way to Moscow or Leningrad. **Japan** has more small companies than almost any other country. *Italy* produces dancers rather than companies, directors rarely lasting long in the emotionally-overcharged atmosphere of theatres such as La Scala. **Germany** has numerous opera houses, many with a small ballet company. Hamburg has its resident giant, John Neumeier, doing his own, idiosyncratic thing. Loved by many, he is received with indifference by others. His ballets such as *Dame aux Camellias* or *Amleth (Hamlet)* are often excessively literary at the expense of the dance, but always intensely theatrical. **South Africa** has supported three big companies, though a lot of their native talent *jetéd* to Britain in the 1950s.

TERRINE DE BALLET
(Potted History)

The true ballet bluffer does not really need to know any ballet history at all. It is highly unlikely that in-depth historical analysis will take place even in such a temple of ballet worship as the amphitheatre of the Royal Opera House. Ballet is a *now* art much concerned with current favourites and fancies, but a few salient facts might help if you are taken by a desperate urge to up-stage a particularly persistent know-all (or fellow bluffer) or to understand the occasional historical reference by a critic with academic pretensions.

Ballet at Court

Ballet, a mannered and fussy art form at the best of times, not surprisingly had its origins in the small courts of Italy in the early 16th century.

These court entertainments were taken to France in the middle of the 16th century as part of the baggage of **Catherine de Medici** when she married Henri II. She employed **Beaujoyeux** as her dancing master to organise the great court entertainments arranged to divert her three sons while she ran the country. Her greatest creation, and the only one bluffers need know about, was the *Ballet Comique de la Reine* of 1573. But beware. These **ballet de cour** were not ballets as we know them today. They were spectacles lasting hours and involving soldiers marching in formation, exotic animals, singing, verse, horse ballets and, not least of all, food. They were much more like the opening of the Los Angeles Olympics than a ballet.

Louis XIV, nicknamed the *Sun King* after his role at the centre of the *Ballet de la Nuit*, is the one who can be said to have put ballet on the world stage. From his first dance steps at the age of 12 he became an accomplished dancer and his interest led him to create the **Royal Academy of Music** (1661) and the **Royal Academy of Dance** (1671) in Paris, to formalise steps and style. Over the centuries the Academy developed into the **Paris Opéra** of today. Purist ballet bluffers may ask if this was a good thing.

At roughly the same time in Russia, **Peter the Great** promoted things French in the hope that they would civilise his courtiers. Russian costume was forbidden and dancing was introduced to court. From this, and the forming of an **Academy of Dance** by the Empress **Anna Ivanovna** in 1738, grew the mighty court ballet of the Tsar. Purist ballet bluffers generally consider this is a good thing.

Bring on the Ballerina

The rise of the ballerina is in direct proportion to the rise of her hemline. Note that the first true ballerina was **Marie de Camargo** at the beginning of the 18th century, and that when she raised the hem of her hooped dress to show off her nifty footwork, it was the first step in the upward rise of skirts, and therefore, ballet. **Marie Sallé** wore revealing classical draperies in **Pygmalion** in the decadent London of 1734. Dresses then shortened to the romantic tutu, the short classical tutu, painted body tights and eventually, in Nederlands Dans Theater's *Mutations*, vanished altogether.

Men on the Stage

By the middle of the 18th century ballet was hampered with masks, singing, speech, cumbersome costumes, and stories restricted to kings and queens, gods and goddesses, nymphs and a few shepherds. **Jean**

Georges Noverre proposed some radical changes, and **Dauberval** got the message and choreographed *La Fille Mal Gardée*, the first story of everyday country folk. It has been running ever since.

Italian, **Salvatore Vigano** took up these ideas, having established himself at La Scala in Milan after inheriting a fortue from an admirer. Dancers still hit lucky this way, and if they don't inherit fortunes, they often marry them. But it was one of his young colleagues, **Carlo Blasis** who wrote the definitive guide to technique, *The Code of Terpsichore*. It is from his teaching that the present day classical vocabulary comes. He also devised the *attitude* pose.

Men had a bit of a come back in the late 18th century with **Gaetano Vestris** jumping higher than anyone else, earning the title 'God of the Dance'. His son, **Auguste**, took over the title and was still able to partner the young **Marie Taglioni**, when he was 75.

The Romantic Era

Taglioni ushered in the new age, performing what is rearded as the first ballet to incorporate the elements of romanticism, handy for any bluffer to know, in the opera *Robert The Devil* by Meyerbeer, in which as the Abbess she led ghostly nuns around moonlit cloisters. Her father, **Filippo**, created *La Sylphide* for her, and soon stages were over-run by sylphs, wilis and naiads in exotic places like Scotland, though bluffers should realise that to judge from the shoes of the period, ballerinas did not stay on their toes for long.

Taglioni's greatest rival was the fiery and temperamental **Fanny Elssler**, famous for her Spanish dance *Cachucha*, and the first Romantic ballerina to visit America where she stayed too long and was fired by the Paris Opéra.

The era also produced **Carlotta Grisi**, who was

the first Ondine, and **Lucille Grahn**, for whom Bournonville created his version of *La Sylphide*. These three ballerinas joined Taglioni in London in 1845 for the last great performance of the Romantic era, the famous *Pas de Quatre*. Coping with four mega-stars was almost too much for Benjamin Lumley, manager of Her Majesty's Theatre where the event was staged. Faced with the problem of who should appear top of the bill Lumley simply said 'Let the oldest have the honour.'

Russian Revolt

When French dancer **Marius Petipa** arrived in Russia, the Imperial Ballet was constructed just like the court, culminating with **Kshessinska**, the absolute prima ballerina assoluta, who wore real jewellery for performances. Mere prima ballerinas included the Italians, **Virginia Zucchi**, **Pierina Legnani**, the first Swan Queen, and **Carlotta Brianza**, the first Aurora. (Bluffers should note that when *The Sleeping Beauty* was revived almost fifty years later she mimed the role of the bad fairy.)

The revolt against the rigid Imperial Ballet was first expressed in articles in *Mir Isskusstva* (The World of Art) by **Serge Diaghilev** (Theatre magazine editor), the designer **Alexander Benois** (who once cooked and ate one of Taglioni's pointe shoes) and the painter **Leon Bakst**.

Diaghilev had ideal qualifications for an artistic director; he didn't dance, compose, design or choreograph. By 1909 his **Ballet Russe** was mounting seasons in Paris with such works as *Scheherezade*, *Prince Igor*, *The Firebird* and *Petrouchka*. Equally important, he introduced the very modern (for the time) music of **Stravinsky**, the striking designs of painters such as **Gontcharova**, the dancing of **Anna**

Pavlova (the greatest ballerina of the age), and the oriental-looking sensation, **Vaslav Nijinsky**.

Nijinskymania

Born in 1888, Nijinsky became involved with Diaghilev (like father and son is the usual euphemism) and joined him in Paris after being dismissed from the Imperial Ballet for not wearing the obligatory extra shorts over his tights. There he astounded audiences with his dancing and choreography until marriage to **Romola Pulsky** led Diaghilev to dispense with his services. He gave his last performance as Petrouchka in 1917 and spent over 30 years in mental homes before dying in London in 1950, where he was buried. (Later **Serge Lifar**, another Diaghilev protégé, had Nijinsky's body removed to Paris so that he could be buried alongside it. Such ego.)

Cocktail Time

In the 1920's, having produced a stream of great ballets, Diaghilev found himself, in his own words 'a bartender mixing cocktails'. He tried every sort of exotic brew: Nijinska's smart ballets, Balanchine's early experiments such as *La Chatte*, and Jean Cocteau-inspired confections. The effort exhausted him. A prediction that he would die on water had kept him at home when Nijinsky sailed off to South America and marriage. Ironically, in 1929, he died on holiday in Venice.

Skilled bluffers can make much of the fact that while Diaghilev changed the face of ballet during his life, it was his death (and thus the break-up of his company) that scattered dancers worldwide, the seeds from which today's mega-industry has grown.

BALLET MAKERS

Certain choreographers are in a class of their own. Not only have they produced a huge number of great ballets, but these ballets have in turn influenced generations of other choreographers. There will be little argument between bluffers as to who should fall into this category. It is when discussing the second division that questions arise. Individual taste inevitably means that experienced bluffers will simply insist that an 'also-ran' should be considered an 'all-time' because they have seen some obscure early work, or feel that their candidate has been unfairly neglected by press or managements. Such idle speculation can be most stimulating.

All-Time Greats (strictly alphabetical)

Ashton (1904-1988)

The irreplaceable Sir Fred, OM, CH, CBE, Ecuadorian born choreographer whose countless masterpieces are a potted history of British ballet and whose curtain calls were an art-form in themselves. He made versions of classic stories such as *Cinderella* created in 1948 for the beautiful red-headed and red shoe'd ballerina Moira Shearer and in which he and Sir Robert Helpmann were a monstrous pair of Ugly Sisters. Other hallmark works include:

Façade – Sir Fred at his elegant and wittiest best. Now over 55 years old it sparkles as much as William Walton's tunes, the Popular Song epitomising the weary camp world of the thirties.

Symphonic Variations – Pure geometry in motion, to César Franck's score, created in 1946. Bluffer's can go over the top with similes, celestial spheres and so on, specially if they saw the original cast, Fonteyn, May, Shearer, Somes, Shaw, Danton.

Ondine – In its original version saw the light of day in 1843 with choreography by Jules Perrot. Sir Fred created his version for Dame Margot Fonteyn to Hans Werner Henze's score in 1958. From the original the only idea retained was the *pas de l'ombre* in which Ondine sees her shadow for the first time. One of Fonteyn's greatest roles, it's a classic story of a mortal torn between love for his earthly fiancée and a supernatural being (see *La Sylphide*) and has the usual tragic ending. In this case Ondine warns Palemon that if they kiss he'll die. They do. He does.

La Fille Mal Gardée – Always '*Fille*' to its friends, dates from 1789 when staged in France by Dauberval. 171 years later Ashton unveiled his version. Pure unadulterated pleasure. Sir Fred used every British theatre tradition he could to tell the very French story of Lisa and her lover Colas and the problems they encounter (principally Lisa's mother, Widow Simone) before they can marry. There's a ribbon dance or two, a clog dance, a dance around the maypole, a dance with wine bottles and a live horse. The cock and hens are played by dancers, but in *Les Deux Pigeons*, Ashton's next ballet, he used two well-trained doves. *Fille*'s title defies catchy translation in spite of a competition once initiated by Madam to find one.

The Dream – One of Ashton's gems, but the practised bluffer will know it as the vehicle for launching the great Sibley/Dowell partnership in 1964. Set to Mendelssohn's music it is charmingly designed by the modern master of charming design, David Walker, who has worked similar wonders on Ashton's *Cinderella*, Mary Skeaping's *Giselle* and Peter Schaufuss's *La*

Sylphide. 25 years later Sibley still shines as Titania.

Out of a host of other works, bluffers should rave about *Monotones I* and *II*, heavenly geometry again (see *Symphonic Variations*), *A Month in the Country*, which provided a great role for Lynn Seymour, and *Rhapsody*. Bluffers have to affect that they were at the first-night, which was the Queen Mother's birthday, to see Misha and Lesley (Collier) and the showers of rose-petals. Sir Fred was the master of the *pièce d'occasion* having previously mounted a beautiful solo for Dame Margot Fonteyn using steps from all the ballets he created for her (even the most assiduous bluffer was severely challenged to identify them all). He also created a small gem for Her Majesty the Queen's sixtieth birthday gala which will probably never be seen again. It brought to life the famous photograph of Elizabeth and Margaret as children and was inspired by a glimpse Sir Fred had, from the top of a bus, of the two young princesses playing in their garden over fifty years ago.

Balanchine (1904–1983)

The 'all-American' choreographer from Georgia – Russia. The inimitable Mr B. creator of the all-American high-stepping ballerina. His association with Stravinsky was legendary; the Stravinsky Festival of 1972 was a high-point of American ballet. Wearing his cowboy string tie and toggle and boots, he looked as though he had stepped out of his own ballet, *Square Dance*. Latterly a specialist in plotless ballets which are pure movement, a few of his other key works include:

Apollo – Originally entitled *Apollon Musagète* was created in 1928 and established neo-classicism (see Introduction). It shows the birth and youth of Apollo and his instruction of the muses of poetry, mime and dance. Dance wins hands-down before he ascends to Olympus to join the other Gods. Celestial music by Stravinsky.

Serenade – The first ballet Mr. B. created when he went to the United States in 1934. It was made for students of the newly-formed School of American Ballet and premièred in White Plains, New York State. Bluffers should know that incidents which happened during its creation; a dancer falling, another arriving late, were kept in the finished version which closely follows the structure of the music, Tchaikovsky's Serenade in C.

Four Temperaments – Known as *Four T's*, is a melancholic, sanguinic, phlegmatic and choleric ballet created in 1946 for the forerunner company of the New York City Ballet. Like many Mr B. ballets the original décor has long gone, and it is danced, to Hindemith's score, in practice clothes.

Bournonville (1805–1879)
Denmark's biggest export after Carlsberg and ham, trained in Denmark and Paris with his father, Antoine. He made his debut at the Paris Opéra in 1826, and returned to Denmark to become leading dancer for twenty years. His ballets convey moral messages in an appealing way, reflecting the motto which is over the stage at the Royal Theatre 'Ej blot til lyst' (Not only for amusement). He discovered the sixteen-year-old Lucille Grahn to be his Sylph, and quite possibly much more.

La Sylphide – Choreographed in 1836 has outlived the original Paris production of 1832, never having been out of the repertoire of the Royal Danish Ballet for long. There is much discussion as to what has changed about it over the years, but you would be safe to pronounce, as the Bournonville expert Erik Aschengreen does, "The only authentic performance is the first". General opinion is that with the strengthening of the male role in recent years, to equal that of the Sylph, the ballet is as authentic as it should be after 110 years. Bournonville could not afford to pay for the original music (by Schneitzhoeffer) so he commissioned the young Herman Lovenskjold to write it anew (humming a few of the original tunes to inspire him), which he did triumphantly.

Far From Denmark – or Danes at Sea, is one of the Bournonville ballets which hasn't travelled – yet. Whether this tale of sailors from a Danish frigate anchored off Argentina will become as well-loved as *La Sylphide* is a matter for conjecture. It contains a host of national dances, for eskimoes, chinese, indian temple dancers and red indians all of which, like his 'nigger dance' need to be performed with great period style to avoid falling foul of the race relations legislation.

Kermesse in Bruges – High on the list of ballets which will sweep the world – one day. Lucky bluffers will have seen it in Copenhagen danced by the Royal Danish. The title, The Fair At Bruges, is a non-starter. Three brothers set out to make their fortune, bearing with them three gifts from a merchant grateful to them for saving his daughter. One is given a magic ring which makes him irresistible to women; one (Adrian!), is given a sword which makes him invincible; while the third is given a lute which makes everyone dance – shades of Salad Days. After many hilarious exploits the secret of the brothers' success gets out and the elder two and the merchant are arrested for sorcery. Just as the trio are about to be burned at the stake who should come along but the youngest and his magic lute. He makes everyone dance till they are exhausted (Look at me, Oh, look at me, Oh, look at me, I'm dancing. . .) and beg him to stop playing. He agrees, if his brothers can go free and all ends, as they say, with general rejoicing. Completely idiotic stories like this make ballet worthy of serious study.

Napoli – Bluffers will already know the story or at least will have seen the last act divertissement, the only pas de six to be danced by ten.

Fokine (1880–1942)
Mikhail, dancer and then choreographer with the Imperial Ballet, trained at the Maryinsky, and was the key choreographer with Diaghilev. He then produced his ballets for the various singular Ballet Russe companies which tried to keep the Diaghilev tradition alive.

Les Sylphides – Not to be confused with 'La'. Positively soporific in some versions, this is the one about the poet, large floppy bow at throat, and his reverie in the woods. It is danced to Chopin tunes and was originally entitled *Chopiniana* – indeed still is in Russia.

Le Spectre de la Rose – A young girl is asleep in her room after her first ball. She clutches a rose and dreams that its spirit dances with her, before taking a soaring leap out into the night. Created in 1911 for Nijinsky and Karsavina it takes equally great artists to avoid it drifting into embarrassing silliness. The music is Weber's Invitation to the Dance.

Petrouchka – Spell it how you like, was created in 1911 for Nijinsky. Karsavina was the Ballerina and Orlov was the Moor. It provides a great central role always cast from company stars, when in fact it can be more effectively danced by a good character dancer. The Magician manipulates his puppets for the benefit of the audience, but when the curtain comes down the dramas of the triangular relationship of Petrouchka, Ballerina and Moor continue with tragic consequences. Just like life in the average ballet company.

Ivanov (1834–1901)

Worthy of inclusion in the pantheon of the greats on the strength of one and a half ballets, one of which is largely lost. He joined the Imperial Ballet in St Petersburg in 1852, and spent much of his career under the shadow of Petipa who took credit for much of his work. Ivanov created the most potent and powerful image in the world of ballet; the Swan Queen. For his efforts he got little reward in his lifetime and he died penniless and forgotten.

Nutcracker – Petipa's illness during the creation of this ballet in 1892 meant that Ivanov had complete creative control of the Snow Scene and the radiant pas de deux, which is all that is left of his original choreography. Today there are hundreds of different productions worldwide attacking E. T. A. Hoffmann's story and Tchaikovsky's music in as many ways. The ballet has suffered of late from an excess of psychological interpretation and bluffers should manifest the hope that the pendulum will swing back to simpler productions.

Swan Lake – Petipa did the grand court scenes, but it is to Ivanov that we must be grateful for the seminal images of the Swan Queen and her swan maidens in the second and fourth lakeside acts. The popular image of ballet.

Petipa (1818–1910)

The absolute monarch of the Tsar's Imperial Ballet for almost thirty-five years was born in Marseilles. He had a considerable career as a dancer in his father's company in Brussels and at the Comédie Française dancing with Carlotta Grisi. He produced over 60 ballets and created the classic style which is the basis of ballet today.

Don Quixote – A full-length ballet which has little to do with the Don and a lot to do with Basilio, a barber, and his love, Kitri. Created in Moscow in 1869 to thumping tunes by Minkus, the Lloyd-Webber of 19th century ballet music. The pas de deux from the last-act wedding celebrations is a gala favourite giving otherwise tasteful dancers a chance to show off insufferably.

La Bayadère – Choreographed in 1877 to some made-to-measure tunes by Minkus. Only the Kingdom of the Shades scene is seen with any regularity outside Russia today. The famous entry of the temple dancers performing arabesque penchée followed by a back bend, filling the stage, is one of the most spectacular images in ballet. Bluffers scarcely need to know that it is a tale of jealousy and lust in a Rajah's court which culminates with Nikiya, the temple dancer, being presented with a basket containing a poisonous snake to dispose of her which leaves Solor, her lover, free to marry the Rajah's daughter. As *Cléopatre* is no longer in the repertoire, this must now be the biggest asp disaster in the ballet world.

The Sleeping Beauty – Created in 1890, Tchaikovsky's music was not appreciated, and all the Tsar could bring himself to say was 'Very nice'. Now one of the three jewels of the classical crown, bluffers will always refer to it as '*Beauty*'.

Swan Lake – Only half Petipa, the court scenes and national dances. What more is there to say about this, the ultimate ballet, except that bluffers should always refer to it as '*Lac*'. This bit of its French title has stuck.

Raymonda – Petipa's last great ballet, made in 1898, five years before his retirement, to ravishing music by the famous chemist, Glazunov. The story is so incredibly complicated that it is rarely performed complete outside Russia. The last act, the wedding celebrations of Raymonda and her Crusader lover, Jean de Brienne, is a glorious cascade of classical and Hungarian dance justifying what has gone before, which was... Raymonda loves Jean who is always crusading. He sends her, in lieu of a postcard, a tapestry of himself. But Abderame, a Saracen, tries to seduce her in the meantime. After momentary temptation she spurns him and is rewarded by the appearance of a ghostly White Lady who conjures up a vision of Jean. But Abderame will not take no for an answer and tries to abduct her. Fortunately Jean and King Andrew II of Hungary, no less, arrive in the nick of time to rescue her. The King orders Jean and Abderame to fight for Raymonda, but when it looks as though the Saracen will win, the White Lady intervenes again to ensure that true love wins in the end.

Modern Masters

Béjart (b. 1922)

To the masses, a master of stagecraft and significance; to others a choreographer of hidden shallows. Arlene Croce of the New Yorker expressed serious opinion perfectly; 'pronounce his name Beige Art'. Born in Marseilles, his early choreography was regarded as avant-garde in the fifties. His company developed into the Ballet of the Twentieth Century in 1960, based at the Monnaie Theatre, Brussels. Most recent project *The Ring Cycle* as a five-hour ballet. It works! A must.

Le Sacre du Printemps – Keynote ballet made in 1959,

already showing the direction his future would take. Male parts predominate.

Ninth Symphony – Beethoven's, used to create a hymn for mankind. Multi-racial sentiments using oriental, asian and black dancers.

Boléro – Uses the music written for Ida Rubenstein by Ravel, but made more famous by Torvill and Dean on ice. Originally created for a single girl dancing on a huge round table surrounded by men, it has since been performed by a man surrounded by women and, latterly, by a man surrounded by men. O tempora, O mores.

Cranko (1927–1973)

Born in the Transvaal, Cranko was a dancer, and very soon a choreographer, with the Sadlers Wells Ballet. Known for his inventive humour in the theatre with his revue *Cranks* in the fifties, as well as in his ballets. Became Director of the Stuttgart Ballet in 1961 and formed a major company (see Companies). Died on a plane flying from New York to Stuttgart.

Pineapple Poll – Adapted from W. S. Gilbert's Bab Ballad, The Bumboat Woman's Story, the music is Sullivan arranged by Charles Mackerras and the scenery by Osbert Lancaster in his inimitible style, which would later decorate *Fille*. Poll is infatuated by the devastatingly handsome Captain Belaye and is in turn loved by the pot boy, Jasper. Poll and her friends disguise themselves as sailors and board Belaye's ship. But he returns with his bride and her chattering Aunt Dimple. Much confusion ensues, but eventually all are becalmed. Belaye promotes himself to Admiral and as a consolation prize Jasper becomes a Captain. As a result Poll agrees to marry him. She is clearly a social climber.

Onegin – An unsung masterpiece created for the Stuttgart Ballet in 1965. In recent years the role of Tatyana has been passionately danced by Makarova for several of her positively last farewell performances. Music by Tchaikovsky, but not from the opera of the same name. Ballet bluffers should note that Onegin is pronounced 'on-yay-gin' with a hard 'g' and should not sound like an interval drink.

MacMillan (b. 1929)

Sir Kenneth, former Director of the Royal Ballet and now Associate Director with American Ballet Theatre. Born in Dumfermline he forged his father's signature on the application for his first audition. He was a fine dancer with the Sadler's Wells Ballet after studying at its School. Prolific producer of ballets, many inspired by Lynn Seymour, and something of a specialist in full-length story ballets.

The Invitation – Set some time before the First World War, a young girl and her cousin are seduced during a house-party by an unhappy married couple. Started the great partnership of Seymour and Christopher Gable in 1960.

Anastasia – Began life as a one-act ballet in 1967, to music by Martinu, in Berlin. Everyone thought Lynn Seymour sensational in the title role and some thought a three-act ballet was crying to get out. MacMillan obviously agreed as he produced it for the Royal Ballet in 1971. He used Tchaikovsky's Symphonies 1 and 3 for the additional two acts which show the Grand Duchess Anastasia's life at court before she is discovered in a mental home in act three. Everyone thought Seymour sensational. Some thought a one-act ballet was crying to get back in.

Manon – A modern masterpiece created for the Royal

Ballet in 1974, the music is by Massenet, but not from Manon the opera. It is a glorious pot pourri of other works ranging from *Cendrillon* to the sensuous *Valse très lente*, beautifully melded together by Leighton Lucas. Manon is the original good-time girl who, swamped with riches at the beginning, eventually ends up in one. In love with Des Grieux, a poet, she accepts money to live with a rich gentleman, but not before a night of passion and a pas de deux in the poet's bedroom. Manon plans to run away with him, but the gentleman arranges to have them arrested. Manon is sent to a penal colony, the faithful poet following her just in time to rescue her from the amorous intentions of the jailer. Escaping through the swamps Manon catches fever, but summons up enough energy to dance a final pas de deux. Sibley and Dowell triumphed on the first night, with a brilliant characterisation of Manon's brother by David Wall.

Elite Syncopations – A romp created in 1974 at the height of the Scott Joplin craze. Widely performed it is a case of rags to riches for MacMillan.

Massine (1895–1979)

You could say that Leonide Massine should be classed as an all-time great. That he isn't, may simply be a whim of fashion. Born in Moscow, he trained at the Imperial School, joined the Diaghilev enterprise to dance in *The Legend of Joseph* in 1913, and didn't look back. No wonder: he was Diaghilev's principal choreographer and greatest passion. After Diaghilev's death he was associated with the various Ballet Russe companies, becoming noted for his 'symphonic' ballets. Pronounce him the Russian way – Mee-ass-in.

Parade – Cocteau concocted a scenario, in response to Diaghilev's request 'Astonish me!', involving circus performers trying to attract an audience. The cubist décor was by Picasso and the score, by Erik Satie, included passages for a typewriter.

La Boutique Fantasque – Created in 1919 to Rossini tunes orchestrated by Resphigi, it concerns a toy shop in which dolls come to life to help a pair of can-can dancers who have been sold to different families. Apart from an insufferable poodle (bluffers should always pity the dancer cast in this leg-raising part) the ballet is best described as a romp.

Nijinska (1891–1972)
Sister of Nijinsky and Diaghilev's choreographer in the early twenties, she created two key works.

Les Noces – Made in 1923 to a Stravinsky score, as a series of tableaux showing a Russian peasant wedding, designed in sombre browns by Natalia Goncharova, it is an equally sombre and deeply devotional piece. Sir Frederick Ashton brought Nijinska to the Royal Ballet to re-create it some forty years after its first performance.

Les Biches – The epitome of twenties chic (as was her *Train Bleu*) heightened by Poulenc's bright score. It is a little bit naughty with hints of lesbianism. Bluffers should assume that just about everybody remembers how brilliant Svetlana Beriosova was, brandishing a long cigarette holder and swinging her long string of pearls, in the role of the Hostess.

De Mille (b. 1909)
Agnes, niece of Cecil the movie mogul, trained partly with Rambert in London. Her ballets include *Fall River Legend* (Lizzie Borden took an axe ...) and *Rodeo* which together with others such as Loring's *Billy the Kid*, are the first American national ballets.

They led directly to the first serious ballet in a musical; *Laurie makes up her mind* in *Oklahoma*.

Nijinsky (1888–1950)

An all-time great dancer and innovative choreographer, though only one of his ballets is performed today.

L'Après-midi d'un Faune – Made in 1912 it is still danced, long outliving the scandal caused by the use to which the faun put the scarf dropped by a nymph, thus bringing the ballet to a climax. It is also notable for Nijinsky's odd choreographic ideas which involved the dancers walking in profile as though they had stepped down from an Egyptian frieze.

Le Sacre du Printemps – First saw the light of day at the Théatre de Champs Elysées in 1913. Stravinsky's music caused such an uproar that it could hardly be heard by the dancers; Nijinsky had to shout out the complicated rhythms from the wings. As the dancers performed the contorted rhythmic steps a member of the audience shouted 'Un dentiste', another added 'Deux dentistes' after which it was downhill all the way according to Dame Marie Rambert who was there. It is now regarded as a breakthrough in choreography.

Robbins (b. 1918)

Mr Broadway of the ballet. From his first work *Fancy Free* (which became the musical *On the Town*) 'Jerry' has moved easily between the ballet and musical stages. He became Mr B's Associate Director at City Ballet in 1949 and produced a stream of ballets including *The Cage*, *Afternoon of a Faun* and *The Concert*. He choreographed the *Little House of Uncle Tom* ballet in *The King and I* and with *West Side Story* in 1957, changed the course of the musical. His sheer facility has brought praise and some criticism. Usually from those without it.

Afternoon of a Faun – Uses the same Debussy score as Nijinsky's version. The faun is a narcissistic male dancer asleep on the floor of a ballet studio; the nymphs replaced by a ballerina. The gimmick is that the audience is watching the ballet through the rehearsal mirror and that the two dancers only look at each other in the same mirror. The ballerina leaves, the faun awakes. Was it all a dream?

Dances at a Gathering – A plotless ballet to Chopin piano pieces which is a hallmark Robbins' work. Robbins insists it has no plot, but from the moment when the first man puts his hand tenderly on the ground it is clearly a ballet about settlers in a new land. The American experience?

Tudor (1909–1987)
Virtual inventor of the 'psychological' ballet, Antony Tudor started out as general handyman and dancer with the fledgling Rambert company in the thirties. Worked during and after the war in America with Ballet Theatre creating *Pillar of Fire* and *Undertow*. Long fallow periods, but made a triumphant comeback in 1967 with *Shadowplay* for the Royal Ballet. With his sparse and economical style reflected in his private life, it was no surprise that he died in a Buddhist retreat.

Lilac Garden – An archetypal Tudor ballet created in 1936. This taut drama set to Chausson's Poème was a trail-blazing psychological ballet of relationships. The frozen moment in time when the complex emotions of Caroline, her Lover, the Man She Must Marry and the Women in His Past sums up the powerful ballet. Caroline never gets close enough to say goodbye to her Lover until the party is almost over and he puts a sprig of lilac into her hand. But Caroline must marry and she leaves him alone. They'll never gather lilacs in the wings again.

Bluffers will doubtless want to add their own candidates to this list, and there are some with the sort of influence which merit it. You could propose Neumeier for *Midsummers Night Dream*; the double Dutch duo, van Manen and van Dantzig; Kylian; Lavrovsky, creator of the Bolshoi *Romeo and Juliet*; Grigorovich of *Spartacus* fame or the ubiquitous Ronald Hynd whose ballets are danced across three continents.

And then there is the new generation starting with David Bintley, great white hope of British choreography and creator of much-praised works such as *Metamorphosis* and *The Snow Queen* . . .

Anything vous can do, I can do. . .

Remembering who won what and when in ballet competitions is good bluffing material. But you might also question whether the world needs them; **Varna, Moscow, Tokyo, Jackson**, or **Lausanne** (the one to approve of, if you must). And then there's the **European Young Dancer of the Year Award**, a depressing TV event which promotes freaky children who can bore holes in the stage with their *fouettés* and commentating dancers with little to say about their art. Britain can be holier than thou about these circus events, having entered precious few over the years – and won precious little when it has. They are ideal for bravura Russians or the occasional Japanese kamikaze. The Russians expect to win. When Pavlova and Gordeyev won the Moscow prize they didn't even dance in the early rounds and, miraculously, drew best position, (dancing last), when they did.

NAMES TO DROP

Lists of ballet personalities and biographies of dancers are easily come by, but it is always handy to have a few truly obscure alongside the genuinely interesting.

Alicia Alonso – Bluff away that you were present the night she got her sight back mid-performance. Cuban ballerina of Ballet Theatre in the forties and fifties. She now leads the Cuban Ballet and is still performing at 70.

Carina Ari – Swedish ballerina of the short-lived Ballet Suedois, who died in 1970 leaving her fortune (she married into the Bols liqueur family) to a foundation named after her. It cossetts already over-cossetted Swedish dancers. A lot of Bols.

Lord Berners – Eccentric British composer of Ashton's *A Wedding Bouquet*. Had a grand piano in the back of his car and doves painted to match his décor. Full name Gerald Tyrwhitt-Wilson which says it all.

Arlette van Boven – Belgian dancer, former Director of NDT2. Now Artistic Co-ordinator of all three NDT companies. Brilliant administrator, teacher, talent spotter and ballet news gatherer. Pure Leo.

Anton Dolin – Every bluffer has to have a Pat Dolin story. Find yourself one.

Anthony Dowell – Tudor's Boy With Matted Hair, first brought to notice by Erik Bruhn in his production of *Dances from Napoli*. Created CBE in 1973 with expectations of higher things if he can stick it out long enough as Director of the Royal Ballet.

Adam Glushkovsky – Truly a name to bluff with. Dancer and teacher in Moscow and St Petersburg at the beginning of the 1800s. Best known for saving the Moscow Ballet School two days before Napoleon's troops reached the city in 1812.

Beryl Grey – Tall, striking Royal Ballet ballerina who danced her first full-length Swan Lake on her 15th birthday in 1943. As Director of London Festival Ballet from 1968 to 1980 was noted for her double entendres, mostly unprintable.

Robert Joffrey – For years kept his small company together in New York bringing many Ashton ballets to America. One of very few choreographers of Afghan descent, born Abdullah Jaff Anver Bey Khan.

Jules Léotard – French acrobat who invented the rehearsal garment which looks like a one-piece bathing costume. Since Jane Fonda, a fashion item.

Serge Lifar – Glamour boy of the Diaghilev Ballet after Dolin. Became architect of French ballet post-Diaghilev, though few of his ballets are performed now apart from *Suite en Blanc*. Founded his own University of the Dance and was prone to give out hand-written diplomas at parties.

Joseph Maillot – Costumier at the Paris Opéra in the early 1800s. Inventor of tights which became widely used. In theatres in the Pope's domain they had to be blue, not flesh-coloured.

Alicia Markova – Diaghilev's 'little English girl' trained by Astafieva in her famous King's Road, Chelsea, studio where fellow student Patrick Healey-Kay pinched her and pulled her hair. Founded London

Festival Ballet with Healey-Kay, by now called Dolin. Directed the Metropolitan Opera Ballet. Tirelessly lectures, teaches and coaches today. A fund of anecdotes, many collected in *Markova Remembers* — a bluffing necessity.

Peter Martins – Co-Director of New York City Ballet since Mr. B's death. Tall elegant dancer from Denmark who took naturally to City Ballet style and helped shape it thereafter. Now choreographing for the company. Not easy, as Mr B. was a hard act to follow.

Charles Mudry – Ballet master extraordinaire. Swiss-born, Russian-trained teacher of a generation of fine young dancers, mostly Swedish. After three years with Neumeier in Hamburg now back with the Swedes. Can say 'cheese' in thirteen languages.

Rudolf Nureyev – Born in 1938, a difficult student and temperamental dancer with the Kirov. Leapt to freedom after great success during the company's visit to Paris in 1961. Became a ballet pop idol in the west. Magical partnership with Fonteyn. Made a whole generation of male dancers pull their jocks up. Has danced everything from the classics to the avant-garde. Staged big productions of erratic quality and has slapped more ballerinas than most, particularly when directing La Scala. Now in farewell tour mode, which may well go on some time.

Anna Pavlova – Took ballet to places no pointe shoe had trod before. In Hollywood she was filmed with Douglas Fairbanks; Frederick Ashton saw her in Peru; and in New Zealand, her name was given to a meringue cake.

Madame Maria Sackova – Ballerina, presumed

Russian, but with rumours of a colonial pedigree. Muse of the legendary Clarke/Crisp writing partnership.

Peter Schaufuss – Every bluffer knows his parents were Frank Schaufuss and Mona Vangsaae of the Royal Danish Ballet. Danish trained he left for Canada aged 17, but was soon back, homesick. But not for long. Joined Festival in 1970 and then City Ballet in 1974. Endless guesting with companies ranging from Pittsburgh to Petit. Mounted award-winning production of *La Sylphide* for Festival in 1978, *Napoli* for the Canadians in 1982. Most famous role; aged six, as the Page in Ashton's *Romeo and Juliet* in 1955. Now directs the Berlin Ballet.

Moira Shearer – Back in the ballet briefly in 1987 in Gillian Lynne's L. S. Lowry ballet, will have a place in any ballet book as the red-headed heroine of *The Red Shoes*. To Dance is to Live.

Paul Taylor – Wonderfully witty modern dance choreographer whose *Aureole* is in the repertoire of many classical companies to give the impression they are progressive.

Stanley Williams – The svengali of male dance teaching and guru to the greats. English born, but brought up in Denmark where he became expert in the Bournonville style. Now teaches at the School of American Ballet (the City Ballet School). His devotees don't travel far without a cassette of his class in their baggage.

Glossary of Characters

A brief run-down of some characters and creatures a bluffer will find in ballet. Anthropomorphism looms large, with only one example of botanomorphism.

Naiads – Water sprites as in *Ondine*.

Dryads – Wood sprites as in *Don Quixote*.

Sylphs – Air sprites as in *La* and *Les*.

Wilis – Girls who die after being jilted before their wedding day. Only recorded sighting is in *Giselle*.

Swans – In the enchanted and dying varieties, with one from Tuonela.

Peri – Guardian of the flowers of immortality and therefore not greatly in demand.

Muses – Mainly ballerinas who inspire, or so it is said, choreographers. As with Fonteyn/Ashton, Seymour/ MacMillan, Haydée/Cranko, Farrell/Balanchine. Or when they make a stage appearance, being instructed by Apollo. Terpsichore is the muse of dance.

Nymphs – Winsome goddesses, an obsession of choreographers over the centuries. A case of nymphomania?

Fauns – Half man, half goat popular in court ballets along with satyrs. Have made only a few afternoon appearances since.

Fairies – In many shapes and sizes in the ballet world; indeed even in some ballets. See *The Dream, Cinderella*, etc.

Dolls – Mechanical – or magical, notably *Coppélia, Boutique Fantasque, Nutcracker*.

Birds – As in Blue and Fire, with different species such as cocks, both farmyard and golden. A couple of pigeons make occasional appearances.

Trolls – Gnomic underground beings of gnarled aspect and dreadfully hearty sense of fun, mainly Danish as in *Folk Tale*, with the odd Norwegian, as in *Peer Gynt*.

Butterflies – Not as many as you might imagine, but some in *Piége de Lumière*, *The Concert* and choreographers' stomachs on opening nights.

Friends – Ballerinas invariably appear with a cohort of identikit friends. The ballerina is the one with the fanciest dress.

Whores – Identified by unkempt hair and a bosom-shaking tendency. Seen a lot in MacMillan ballets.

Courtesans – High-class whores of haughty demeanour, in high society or at court. They usually do lots with their fans. Seen often in MacMillan ballets.

Villagers – Frightfully jolly and healthy young people endlessly folk-dancing, who have obviously managed to avoid the poverty and disease of the period in which their story is set. They live in the tiniest of cottages and make animated conversation about the price of grapes (*Giselle*) or fish (*Napoli*) or the devastating beauty of the ballerina.

Townspeople – As above, but make more sophisticated conversation about the price of whores (*Romeo and Juliet*) and the devastating beauty of the ballerina.

Bayadères – Indian temple dancers with a penchant for penchées. See *La Bayadère*.

Corsaires – Pirates from the north coast of Africa with a penchant for gold lamé trousers.

Danseur noble – A male dancer of the princely type who wouldn't be seen dead appearing as any of the above creatures, but might not object to being a dancing rose.

Poets – Found mooning in the shrubbery suffering from sylphilis as in *Les Sylphides* or having drug-induced fantasies chasing their muse as in Ashton's *Apparitions* or Massine's *Symphonie Fantastique*.

Queens – Often found at the ballet, as well as in them. Degrees of royalty vary from full-blown as in *The Sleeping Beauty* to minor such as the Princess Mother in *Swan Lake*, along with the bad-tempered Queen of the Wilis in *Giselle*.

THE AUTHOR

Craig Dodd has been involved with the ballet as critic, biographer, sometime agent and general busybody for over twenty-five years. Hailing from North Wales, where ballet was regarded as a dubious business, he plunged into the ballet world on arrival in the fleshpots of London. His breakthrough into criticism involved writing a piece after the first ballet performance he saw, posting it to the now-defunct *Ballet-Today,* and waiting for it to be published. It was. A similar ploy worked with *The Guardian* and *The Dancing Times*.

He has written fourteen books, total sales of which are well in excess of one million, which you could never tell from his bank balance. For light relief from the serious business of the ballet, he has started an enterprise in the ultimate bluffing business, public relations.

THE BLUFFER'S GUIDES

Available at £1.95 and (new editions) £1.99 each

Accountancy
Advertising
Antiques
Archaeology
Ballet
Bird Watching
Bluffing
British Class
The Classics
Computers
Consultancy
Cricket
EEC
Espionage
Feminism
Finance
Fortune Telling
Golf
Green
Hi-Fi
Hollywood
Japan
Jazz
Journalism
Literature

Management
Marketing
Maths
Modern Art
Motoring
Music
Occult
Opera
Paris
Philosophy
Photography
Poetry
Public Speaking
Publishing
Racing
Seduction
Sex
Teaching
Television
Theatre
Top Secretaries
University
Weather Forecasting
Wine
World Affairs

All these books are available at your local bookshop or newsagent, or can be ordered direct from the publisher. Just tick the titles you require and fill in the form below. Prices and availability subject to change without notice.

Ravette Books Limited, 3 Glenside Estate, Star Road, Partridge Green, Horsham, West Sussex RH13 8RA.

Please send a cheque or postal order, and allow the following for postage and packing: UK 27p for one book and 15p for each additional book ordered.

Name ....

Address...

....

....